Convert Your Cozy Home into a Money-Making Factory

Tips on Starting Your Own Profitable Home Business

By: Nancy Hall

9781635019933

I0510835

PUBLISHERS NOTES

Disclaimer – Speedy Publishing LLC

Speedy Publishing LLC

40 E Main Street, Newark, Delaware, 19711

Contact Us: 1-888-248-4521

Website: http://www.speedypublishing.co

REPRINTED Paperback Edition: 9781635019933:

Manufactured in the United States of America

DEDICATION

To Daniel – you will never know how much I love you.

TABLE OF CONTENTS

CHAPTER 1- ACTING ON THE DESIRE TO START A HOME BUSINESS

There's a difference between having the interest to establish a home business and being able to do home business. Before you quit your line of work and begin a home business you ought to first ask yourself assorted questions.

The first thing that you're supposed to do is be realistic before you consider setting things up and creating your home business. Have some ample time and ask yourself assorted simple questions. The first question that's supposed to be in your mind before you start a home business is whether you are ready to start.

Having self-assurance is very important when it comes to business and without assurance you cannot go far. For a home business to start you must believe that it is going to flourish.

You ought to likewise ask yourself whether the rest will have an idea that you are a main contender for self-employment. There are times once we are a small bit over confident about our ability.

Convert Your Cozy Home Into a Money-Making Factory

Once you begin thinking of whether you are going to be successful in home business or not, you must be honest with yourself.

Think about the way you work at your work place and ask yourself whether you complete your work regardless the situation. You ought to likewise ask yourself whether you always work hard in the presence or in the absence of your boss. The minute you answer these questions or you do an assessment of yourself through these questions then you're ready to begin.

The other thing that you ought to ask yourself is whether or not you have ever attended any forum or taken classes of starting and controlling a small business. If you have not then it is best that you do before you begin.

This will help you know the pros and cons of a home business. You ought to likewise be ready to go down in your standards of living as the business is progressing. Home businesses are a good thing but most of the small businesses begin with a lot of work but make very small profit. And so you ought to ensure that you've some amount of money someplace to add on the small profit.

The additional thing is that you ought to be prepared to work very long hours with very small profit at the end of the day. This is how the business starts out. It doesn't flourish the minute you have started it you have to work hard and be patient. Make certain that you likewise have acquired the right legal documents before you begin a business.

What is the Right Foundation to Success?

In order to build your own success you have to bear the correct foundation.

What does success mean to you? For a couple of individuals, being successful merely entails having a lot of income. While for a few other people, being successful means experiencing a beneficial relationship, fine health or doing a bang-up job in a career.

Regardless how you specify success, there must be a basic definition deep in your brain. You comprehend precisely what you wish to achieve in your life story. And if you achieve it in your life story, you will be considered a success.

Before you are able to achieve the success you desire in your life story you need to understand the core factor that specifies what you do to make you successful. It is this core element that will drive you into making the correct decision and taking the right action.

And this core factor is your burning desire. You first of all need to have an idea of what you desire or what you wish in your life story. If you do not even understand what you desire in your life story, how are you going to achieve it?

Once you have discovered what you really and truly wish to achieve in your life story, just implement these four easy steps in some manner and your dreams will have a better chance of coming true.

- Build up and beef up your belief system. You have to trust it before you can achieve it. If you wish to become a millionaire and drive a BMW 5 Series, then trust that it is imaginable for you to achieve it first.

- The 2nd step is to set a clear goal. Goal setting is among the most powerful tools that can help you to achieve what you wish in your life story. Write down your goals on a piece of paper, carry it everyplace with you and review your goals day-to-day.

Acquire strategies on how you are able to achieve your goals. Goals will keep you focused on your road to your success; strategies are what you need to acquire in order to make your goals come true. Sit down and brainstorm for a minute, think about what strategies and action steps you need to take to make your goals come true.

- Take uniform action according to your strategies. Once you have written down your goals and your strategies, take massive and uninterrupted action day-after-day. The key here is consistency and persistence. You will discover yourself moving closer toward your goals each and daily.

By following all of the 4 steps mentioned above, you will be able to achieve whatever you wish in your life story. And don't forget that you need to discover what you really wish to achieve in your life story before you are able to achieve it. Find out the burning desire that keeps you going and you will finally achieve the great success that you wish.

Chapter 2- How to Start a Home Business

Many individuals right now are sick of running to a daily job of 9 in the morning to 5 in the evening and so they're seeking best home businesses.

There are numerous home businesses and the only thing that you have to do is to look around and get the correct business ideas. Running your own home business has got lots of benefits compared to working for somebody else's business.

One of the benefits is that your schedule is more flexible. This is because you get to work at whatever time that you wish and likewise at the comfort of your own home. This is really nice as you've time for your loved ones and friends as compared to being an employee.

With home business you are able to make as much income as you want depending on the hours that you spend in it, the effort that you put in and many other crucial factors of success.

With home business, there are no bosses to follow you around and holler at you for every slight error; you become your own boss. Being your own boss means that you ought to be able to produce more and bring out high quality work. Because of the introduction of the net and websites, it is now possible to search for different and many home business ideas online today.

The first thing that you ought to ask yourself before beginning your home business is what your area of expertise is. There are a lot of things that one may do including cooking and sewing. The minute you discover your area of interest or whatever you're good at then coming up with your business becomes much easier.

There are those individuals who are specialists in baking and likewise decorating cakes for special events, this may be an idea for you. There are likewise others who know how to bake assorted types of cakes. They likewise may have recipes for the different sorts of cakes and this could be something that has been passed down. This could be a really good home business if done properly.

There are likewise those who understand how to sew. You are able to easily do a business of plain sewing or even embroidery. The only thing that you'll be required to do is to buy the assorted materials or tools. Then all you have to do is utilize your creativity to come up with assorted designs and colors of embroidery. You are able to sell this as covers for sofas, tables, cushions and likewise pillow covers.

Nancy Hall

The point is whatever you are good at can become a home business.

Selling Data Products: Cheap to Produce, Costly to Sell

Data products are the Internet-age term which implies the publication of data-rich material on the net. This material may take any form, but broadly when we speak about data products, we're talking about eBooks, e-zines, videos, audio-books and the like.

Generally, this is material that people may download and store on their hard disk and withdraw it afterwards according to their convenience. There's one more common strand running through all the data product devices - they have to furnish advantageous content to the user.

There are 2 ways in which you're able to get into the data merchandise business:-

You might produce the data content yourself or outsource it to someone so that you have your own merchandise to distribute. You might promote another person's merchandise on your site or blog. Either way, you're doling out informative material.

One of the ways to give out this material is through affiliate promoting. If you're going to market products of others, you might select the available products from an affiliate network and distribute it through a service like AdWords.

In this case, you would not have to have your own site or blog even. All the same, you might likewise distribute such merchandise directly. Selling makes an awesome option if your merchandise is great quality. Utilizing strategies like SEO, viral promoting, social networking and such, you might establish a brand presence for your merchandise and gather a market for it. Once that is produced, you'll discover that your merchandise starts earning for you an everlasting stream of income.

If you carry your own merchandise, there are a lot more advantages. Number one, people associate you with somebody who's an authority in the subject. Your name in the byline means a lot for your believability.

This will ensure that your additional products get a niche for themselves too. Now, bearing your own merchandise doesn't mean that you have to sit and produce stuff on your own. You could outsource work really easily.

Achieve the maximum mileage out of your data merchandise enterprise. If you're looking to stick to your internet home business for a long time, you'll have a presence on the internet, and nothing works better than data products for that.

Never undervalue the might of software applications. You're utilizing dozens of them on your desktop yourself. Software might make you wealthy... really wealthy.

Membership sites might lead in a lot of people through the door of your internet business. Selling software packages is among the most forceful routes to make awesome income on the internet.

With broadband internet, it has become so very simple to supply software in downloadable formats. You market a link from where people might download a particular software package and allow them to access it when they make payment. They'll pay and you provide them the link to download the package.

A lot of marketers tease people by presenting them demo versions of the software for free. This lets the downloaders comprehend the caliber of the merchandise before they choose to buy.

These demo versions typically have a few features locked or they're timed demos which expire after an hour's worth of utilization or so. When that occurs, people are prompted to purchase the merchandise to take advantage of it limitlessly.

People on the internet like each and every sort of software. There's a niche for everything on the internet. So, if you've made an application that will help granny recall her recipes or made software that will help a businessman with his end-of-the-year accounting, you're going to find persons who will be willing to download that and check it out. The success rests in the promoting.

You don't have to have your own software application either. You might purchase the resell rights of software and sell it. There are a lot of creative people on the internet who like building software but don't like the promotion aspect of it. These people give away the software they've developed for a price.

You're able to modify these packages to an extent and in some cases you're able to rebrand them too. Naturally, you sell them at a much higher price than you purchased it for.

Membership sites are merely what their name suggests - these are sites where you're asking people to become members of a site and in return you're supplying them with a host of value-added services.

The general concept of a membership site is that you keep your products hidden from the basic internet public and allow them access to it only if they've taken the membership action that you ask them to. This action might be filling in an internet form, with or without payment, authoring an email to you to express their desire to join the site and so on.

However, you have to comprehend that membership sites do take effort. You have to have a unique concept to make your membership site a hit and you have to make regular efforts to provide superior material to your members.

The internet has a market for everything. Even for your own services. If you believe you're great at something, the internet may be the most beneficial place for you to sell your skills. There are people seeking all sorts of services on the internet.

The jobsites have made the internet a closer market than any other. People are seeking services, and suppliers of these services are seeking people who they might sell the services to. The right collaboration might mean a lot of cash to you.

Naturally, it's understood that the sort of services that have a demand on the internet are services that you are able to supply online. These are by and large services related to site building and promoting. The following services are much desired:-

• Material creation

• Blog management

• SEO

• Site creation

• Social networking services like Craigslist postings

• Handling other virtual staff

• Proofing and editing

The drawback here is that you must spend time. You have to be at your desktop for all the time that you're returning money, which is a really different matter from other approaches like affiliate promoting. You earn simply as much as you work and there's no scope for residual revenue.

Networking is another way and is where you establish a network of people and jointly you market a merchandise or service. At the same time, you attempt to bring more people into the network.

For every individual that joins the network, the upline members pull in a commission. Direct sales take in the cash too, but the chief commission is brought in through the commissions that the network building returns. However, the execution isn't quite as easy. The drawback is that there are many players in the network promoting (likewise called MLM) world.

As well, you have to especially be beware of pyramid systems in which people take in money only by building a network but don't have any merchandise to distribute.

Chapter 3- Interest in the Business Equals Knowledge

We all comprehend that aptitude and disposition is essential when you take on a business. However, it's more essential to have the disposition because knowledge might still be worked at. If you're not interested with a certain opportunity, it's likely that you'll get tired of doing matters repeatedly and you'll want to quit later on, leading you to failure in your business.

If you do like it, it's likely that you would also be able to produce awesome quality without having to exert too much effort. After which, your employer ought to be satisfied, acquire more of your work and then you succeed in your business.

The correct balance is required for progress.

Work might often get in the way of the matters you wish to accomplish in life. As a matter of fact, it is only when individuals retire that they're able to accomplish what they've always wanted to accomplish, however never had the luxury of time and cash. If you're working a 9-5, it's unlikely that you've adequate time to spend with your youngsters, your mate, and yourself.

However, everything will shift when you go into business. If you decide to accomplish your work through the Net, you are able to easily work from home without having to wake so early to prepare, eat, dress, and go to the office. You don't have to fret about being caught up with heavy traffic if you remain at home.

Therefore, if you choose to accomplish business on the net you'll have more time to take care of yourself, get an awesome night's rest and take your time. You are able to even manage your time whichever way you want it to.

Just so long as you're able to commit to deadlines and submit your work on time, you'll be able to have the luxury of time to spend for other more significant things like self and loved ones.

While you might believe that your business won't be able to generate as much cash as your 9-5 job would, think again. You're able to still earn as much depending upon how much time you put in.

Now, your mate doesn't have to nag you so much or quarrel with you about not being able to spend time with him or her. Your youngsters will never have to get angry at you for not playing with them. If you're single, you're able to spend more time with your partner, your acquaintances, or yourself and accomplish anything you wish to do.

The Importance of Credibility and Position in Business

In a paragon world, you want your name to be synonymous with whatever product or service it is that you're providing. You want to be the "go to" individual when prospective clients consider "networking" or "best author" or whatever it is you want to be recognized for. It takes time to establish a report in your industry but if you're strategic in your attack, it won't be long before you're the name on everybody lips. So what do you do?

1. Build upon your net presence

Many individuals go to Google as their 1st source when they're seeking something. So it's crucial to build up your net presence. If a prospect searches for you - and you're invisible on Google but they then seek your competition and discover multiple listings, chances are they're going to believe your competitor is more accomplished. Whether or not that's really true, it's the percept they'll form because of your net presence (or deficiency thereof). To build upon your net presence, you may have a blog where you write on matters or hot topics in your business. You can author articles and post them to relevant online sites. Or you can remark on blogs that are read by your target market. It goes without stating that you should see to it that you've the correct search engine optimization for your site and that your site itself is a clear manifestation of your skills and what you provide.

2. Be a speaker at events

Distinguish the sorts of events attended by your target market and offer to address the crowd. Before you get too charged up and think that you're now going to acquire lots of income as a paid speaker, chances are that you're going to have to do a number of gratis speaking gigs before you are able to call for payment. Moreover, if you're obviously lambasting a product or service, or if you're distinctly using the speaking opportunity as a drill in self-promotion, it's improbable you'll be paid. That's all right. See it for what it is - a dandy marketing chance for you to reach your target market. The thing about speaking is that your audience can make a true connection with you as they get to check you out in person and maybe even talk to you after the event.

3. Be clear-cut about what you're an authority on

It may sound obvious but I'm astonished at the number of small business entrepreneurs who don't have lucidity on this. Think of it is as your "elevator pitch". I've heard some business owners drift on for 5 minutes trying to explicate their expertise to me. And at the end I'm none the wiser on what they really do. Don't go into particulars about the number of qualifications you have and the classes you've done. Keep it simple. Tell individuals how you can assist them.

4. Don't be afraid to deliver a view

We don't want your view about everything from the state of the economy to who should win Dancing with the stars. But we do want your view on matters in your industry. After all, you're the authority in this area so behave like one! Don't be afraid to place your view on blogs, opinion columns, letters to the editor etc. You may author articles for industry publications or, more significantly, publications that are read by your target market.

5. Network

It pays to go to networking events. Frequent networking is a must for any business owner, especially if you're fresh to the game. The key here isn't to expect to have piles of sales after your 1st event. I get tired of hearing business owner's state: "yep I went to a networking event but I'm not going back as I didn't get any customers from it." That's just the incorrect attitude. It takes time to establish relationships. After you've been to a few and you begin seeing familiar faces, your face becomes familiar to them likewise. And before too long, individuals begin associating you with your business or expertise. The stunner is that they begin telling others about what you do also! When it comes to positioning yourself as an authority, it takes time. But a good reputation doesn't come out overnight. Put in the time and energy - and the outcomes will be worth it.

Tap the Help of Mentors

Experience is a highly valued element and often sought through the course of any business entity. Using a mentor to help an individual have some idea or measurable bench mark is a positive additive to a business equation. The benefits of having a mentor cannot be emphasized enough.

Mentoring involves the more experienced party extending the relevant knowledge and skill in a particular area to the less experienced individual.

This is supposed to help the lesser experiences individual in more ways than one to understand and emulate some of the good qualities expounded. The following are some of the ideas behind the wisdom in using a mentor:

Mentoring involves the teaching process either directly or indirectly for the purpose of imparting valuable skills or information on a particular topic or area and this is very useful for the novice trying to make some headway into the said field.

Having someone to lean on for guidance and also to steer the individual away from decisions that will negatively impact the business is not only advantages but also sometimes the defining difference between success and disaster for the business.

Sometimes the mentoring experience can go beyond just assistance. This is where the mentor can actually embark upon sharing resources and networks with the novice.

This is certainly a huge help to the individual just starting out in the business field. The development possibilities are boundless with this type of extended help and it also helps to eliminate some of the risks the novice would have otherwise taken.

Using a mentor also helps to introduce a safer learning environment and this also contributes positively to a lower stressful experience.

The risks taken are then done so in a more calculated manner with minimal if any negative repercussions. For the novice this is a very important element as it is also in most cases a very cost effective way of going about the business endeavor.

CHAPTER 4- NETWORK MARKETING AS A HOME BUSINESS

Sound like something you've been through? Regrettably and unhappily, we have all been there haven't we? We've been ostracized by neighbors, friends, even the letter carrier who runs past your house to avoid you when you answer the door.

Dinosaur marketing - that's what we were instructed to do. Everybody is a candidate for your business or products. Everybody. Thank goodness, things have evolved and marketing for your home business has evolved also. No longer is it essential to beat individuals up attempting to convince them to sign up with your opportunity. Reality is, every opportunity out there is unique and everybody has something special. But how do you pull in the individuals to you that truly want what you have?

Get them to come to you. That's correct. Get individuals to come to you by branding yourself as somebody exceptional...somebody who's well-educated in your field and thus, is seen as a leader.

Somebody they prefer to do business with and not somebody who they would like to hightail away from when they come along. We must utilize attraction marketing. We've heard the term many times recently (unless you've been on a deserted island) but not everybody is quite up to speed on what it is and how it goes. Essentially, attraction marketing has the following elements:

•Draw in candidates to you

•Build a Relationship with your candidates with your net content

•Pre-sell with your content - Give 1st, Take 2nd

•Constitute trust and place yourself as an authority with branding

This is the fresh prototype when it comes to selling in today's market. No longer do you have to go after candidates, hoping they'll join your business or opportunity. It's constructing a warm market on the web. The goal is to generate attraction between us and our prospects by supplying value based information that they can utilize in the marketplace. Information that will help them develop their business or their brainpower about home business. It doesn't matter what you write on, as long as you target your market, supply useful info, and establish a relationship with them by continuing to provide this info on an ongoing foundation.

Provide a free e-book, a free newsletter; anything that will get the candidate returning for more as they begin to see you as a leader in your area. Individuals start to know who you are and trust is finally built because of that familiarity. Relationships take time to grow and this is no different. You need to take the time to work on that relationship on-line as contrary to face-to- face but the outcomes can be amazing. The Net provides the chance to reach the masses with a touch. Outmoded marketing calls for a lot of leg work (literally) to establish these relationships and there's no guarantee that these relationships will be individuals who are targeted for your particular market.

With attraction marketing, the key is aiming at the correct audience. Don't try to pitch your opportunity to somebody who has no interest in beginning their own business. Uplines would have you trust that everybody is a candidate. But, everybody is a suspect before a prospect. Don't languish your time with individuals who have no concern. Rather, dive head long into building permanent relationships with individuals who truly want what you have to provide.

Should You Keep Lists?

Your list is the most useful part of your business. Real estate companies have them; financial institutes have them even holiday booking offices have them.

• **The Bad:** I don't mean sitting down and composing a list of all the individuals you know including your hairdressers next door neighbors cousin, people in your iPhone this not a list.

A list is a group of individuals who subscribe to something or make contact and want more info, or have made a purchase and perhaps interested in making another purchase.

Businesses spend a lot of years contributing to and evolving their lists, contacting individuals on their list in the hope of repeat business some sort of communication from the individual that they're staying in touch with. Many business owners couldn't care less if the building burns up as long as they can keep their list; it's literally worth millions of dollars to them. Some business owners really think that they have to construct the biggest list possible and that alone will shovel in a lot of income. Well, here's the truth: You don't need to have a big e-mailing list in order to be fruitful; you can really make a lot of income with a small business e-mail list. What you truly want is a targeted mailing list of purchasers, producing e-mail lists with only volume in mind is a waste of time.

Certainly, it would be great to have a huge list, but it's the caliber of the list that matters, what you truly need is an interested and likely list of buyers whom you can trust that will purchase from you over and over. You can, naturally, grow your list. List building is unquestionably among the most crucial and complicated tasks while running your business, but with the correct list building strategies, it's definitely worth your time and effort.

•**The Good:** Targeted list, more income

It's true what they say about targeted lists and the gravy train. When you have a choice contact list and when you employ the correct strategies to convince your candidates to buy, it will decidedly translate into more sales. Your elemental goal then, is to turn your email marketing list into a lucrative machine.

A targeted mailing list is very cost-efficient; by reaching a specific group of individuals directly you are able to avoid the time cost of sending offers to a lot of individuals who will merely ignore it. Your targeted e-mail list is compiled of individuals who really have a need for your product or service. It likewise helps to tailor your message to a particular group of individuals, making your offer more relevant and perhaps more probable to be read than a message simply sent to just about anybody.

By advertising more effectively to a targeted group of individuals and by utilizing services like Get Response to make segmental lists, you can decidedly accomplish better results while saving time and money. It takes commitment and tenacity to construct targeted lists to eventually get regular buyers of your goods and services. If you center your efforts on constructing a list in your niche, it will help you make you income month after month.

So essentially, while it's good to acquire a big list, your top precedence should be to make certain that your list is targeted. Learn how to gather contact info of targeted and interested prospects that you are able to test to wind up with a list of proven repeat purchasers.

CHAPTER 5- SHOULD YOU CHOOSE A COMPANY OR BUILD ONE?

Choosing the Right Company for Your Network Marketing

In my experience, I've seen several good companies and a lot of bad ones. It's crucial that you choose a good one. Here is a general view of how I measure a company, listed in order of importance:

1. Is the company going to be around long term? No one can be successful in a company that bombs.

2. Does the product sell away from the network? Meaning, are there consumers who will purchase the product that are not going to join the business?

3. Will I be repaid well for my efforts? This has to do with the commission plan.

4. Does the training make a successful business owner? Online home based businesses are some of the biggest revenue opportunities, because you are able to work from home and there's no need to invest crazy revenue in comparison to some offline business. You've the least financial risk when you begin. You can get a proven step by step system that will assure you. In the correct company you'll be surrounded by positive successful individuals who will push and encourage you so it will be easier to succeed.

Here are the main factors in more detail of solid home based business company:

1)The Company

•Seek a solid company that has the correct leadership in place with a good proven track record of past success (seek success stories)

•Sign up with a company where you're like a member of big family and one movement with one destination (produce a success story)

•Make sure there is training from top producers and the best professionals in order to acquire quick and good results

•Discover a company where there is step by step training for newbies

•Utilize common sense

2)The Industry

•It must be something that's red-hot right now and has the major growth potential in the near and remote future

•It must be a fast growing industry

•Realize that the net is the best place to start a business

•Realize that no experience is necessary, because with the right company you'll get full training and become a success

3)The Products (four key elements)

•It has to have worth to the marketplace (no worth = no income)

•Seek high commission products

•Don't forget about the magic of residual revenue

•There should be small commissions products included for quick and continuous sales

4)   The Compensation Plan

•There should be quick revenue for new coming members (little and quick sales)

•There should be a multi-tiered compensation plan = residual revenue (work once and get paid eternally)

•There should be large commissions

5)   The Training and Support

•Regardless how great the product, likely market or company, there must be a suitable support structure in place so everybody gets taken care of

•You should get an answer from your support ticket in less than 48 hours

•The best support is to have a live chat support and the possibility to call the support center

•You should get live training from top producers and marketing authorities

•You must have step-by-step training for newbies

Note: The last detail on the above list deals with training. Training is exceedingly crucial as it sets in motion the activities of the group or organization.

Your Ideas, Your Plans, Your Business

Many people are finding that turning what they do best into a viable business endeavor can be a lucrative and interesting way of churning out a good income. However in doing so, one should be careful in evaluating its benefits and revenue earning power, before making the commitment fairly permanent.

The following are some points that should help in making such an evaluation:

For some people doing what they enjoy bring out the best results in them no matter how hard the matter at hand may be. Therefore it is important to identify anything that the individual enjoys doing and consider it for business purposes.

Attempting to create the possibility of garnering some revenue through setting up a business based on this enjoyment may bring forth pleasantly surprising results.

Evaluating the market against the capabilities and expertise of the individual is also another platform to gauge the relevance of setting up a successful business venture.

It can be a very rewarding and satisfying experience to discover that the individual can charge other for something he or she simply enjoys doing.

This kind of business venture usually has the potential of achieving phenomenal success as the more money made the more the rewarding feelings will be.

Making the elements that bring enjoyment, into a viable business can be done with some professional looking elements included in the equation.

Setting up a proper book keeping system, having a list of possible clients, creating and designing supporting documents that address the professionalism of the business are all part of the setting up exercise.

For most people who venture into business based on their interest or expertise find the whole exercise both exciting and challenging. This encourages the individual to push further and higher to achieve the best possible results.

CHAPTER 6- THE SECRETS TO RUNNING A BUSINESS THAT LASTS

Whether the relationship exists between a customer and sales professional, between a manager and employee, or between two business colleagues, setting up rapport creates the "glue" between individuals.

4 Steps to Rapport in 1 Minute:

1. Discover common denominators

2. Ascertain communication/social style

3. Align personal and professional measures

4. Institute a baseline for constructing trust

Step 1: Discover common denominators.

Many individuals squander the opening seconds when coming across somebody for the first time. You are able to learn a great deal about somebody within the first 15 seconds if you train your eyes and brain to pull in and process the clues around you. Have you ever noted how a suspense novelist or film producer utilizes the opening scene to set the stage and the mood for what follows? The same holds when you're meeting somebody for the first time; your aim is to identify at least one thing that you've in common with that individual.

Step 2: Ascertain communication / social style.

Each of us have a basic preference for processing data and for sharing our views and feelings with other people, which together we refer to as our communication, or social, style. We may pick to connect with other people from our strengths or fall prey to unhealthy triggers, like debilitation, hunger, anger, or tension. Skilled communicators realize when somebody is in their "backup mode" and can take prompt steps to shift h/her to their optimal state. Communication and social style appraisals like MBTI, DiSC, Wilson Learning, and Keirsey Temperament may help you clarify your communication strengths and identify the social styles of other people.

Step 3: Align personal and professional measures.

What you do during the next 15 seconds ascertains whether the initial connection has lasting potential. It calls for you to listen on a deeper level. Learning how to adjust your values isn't about adopting the values of everybody you meet. It's listening for fundamental clues and cues about a person's belief systems and their values. Empathizing with another's core values allows you to produce a bond without necessarily agreeing with their values. Hear the language somebody uses during the conversation. Do they use "thinking" words or mostly "feeling" words? Do they utilize value based words like trust, honesty, ethics, or credibility?

Try to get the individual to describe a value word – you don't want to assume that your definition is the equal.

Step 4: Institute baseline for constructing trust.

Rapport is a basis of trust. When was the last time you did business with somebody where your "gut" told you not do? What was the outcome? Can you think of the process you went through in evaluating their trustworthiness? The intuitive process happens in a blink of an eye! Your brain stores data based on behaviors you've trusted in the past (as well as the times when you didn't). Dragging up previous pain about these attributes and behaviors will frequently translate to a mistrust of an individual, although you can't quite "put your finger" on how come.

TIP: Use the last bit of time to validate whether you've built rapport with the individual, or if you need to return to one of the previous steps for a fast adjustment. Attempting to move a conversation forward before its time, frequently results in a feeling that you're just "going in circles".

Using Rapport to Upsell

If you worry that free samples will result in more tire-kickers than real customers, develop a low-priced, but desirable product or service to sell to your target market. Make certain the product or service is top-grade. Once you've gained the customer's confidence on a small sale, it will be easier to cut down concerns about placing big orders with you.

If the client does not bite on the first attempt to trade up to greater and better sales, don't forget about them. If you have qualified the customer beforehand and know there are good possibilities for additional sales, stay in touch on a regular basis.

Send them news clippings, press releases, product announcements and anything that will help build your case for being a qualified and reliable supplier of products to them. If you aren't trained on effective ways to upsell, chances are you either offend clients by being too pushy, or leave money on the table that customers would have willingly spent with you. Either alternative is costly.

Upselling refers to when you help a purchaser decide to buy a little extra or "up-grade" slightly the final buy. A car dealer, for instance, may inform customers at the time of ordering about upholstery protection and undercoating. A shoe salesperson may suggest that when you buy a pair of shoes that you likewise use some weather protectant spray. These are commonly small purchases that the buyer doesn't have to put a lot of thought into. The incentive is they may be extremely profitable for you as the sales person and for your organization.

Assumed is the key. You've got to assume that the client will naturally want this. Start the upsell with a brief advantage, and then if possible, add something unique about what you're selling. To prevent sounding pushy, particularly if the upsell requires some elaboration, invite the customer's permission to describe it. Here's a case of the wrong way to upsell. Conceive of dining at a restaurant where you've just finished a huge meal. The server asks, "Would you care for dessert? If you say "Yes", you may give the impression of overindulging. So many buyers refuse out of civility. Result - no sale.

So the savvy server doesn't ask if the buyer wants dessert. The pro just assumes that when individuals go out for a meal they're treating themselves. So naturally they'll want to treat themselves to dessert. In this case, the server pulls up the dessert tray and says, "To finish up your meal with a little something sweet, (that's the advantage) I brought the dessert tray over for you. Would you like to hear about the most popular ones?" (Asks permission to proceed) When the buyer agrees to hear about the desserts the server doesn't just list them by name; he names their advantages. So instead of saying, "This is chocolate mousse." Rather he'd say something like, "If you like chocolate you'll love this. We've got a chocolate mousse that melts in your mouth and makes you question what the ordinary individuals are doing today."

Center on buyer needs-not yours. Don't attempt to sell the customer something you wouldn't buy if you were in their shoes. It's totally irrelevant whether or not this leverage suits your needs; what is relevant is whether it suits the customer's. That perspective empowers you to upsell effectively and with unity.

Hands-on demo. Among the most effective upselling techniques is getting the customer to utilize the product in your location. A hairdresser, for instance, may put hair gel in the customer's hand and show them how to apply it themselves. By showing the customer how to get the salon look at home, they produce a value-added upsell.

Group associated products. It's a good thought to group similar add-ons and provide them as an upsell at a package price. If somebody is getting a haircut and you talk to them about shampoo, it only adds up to show them a package deal that groups conditioner and shampoo at a package price.

Bottom line: Every business owner should honestly consider whether or not they could improve the way they up-sell. For most businesses, a little professional training can make a world of difference.

Train to Keep Up with the Trends

Being in business, especially for those who have been in this line of work for a long time, creates a comfort that is often quite enticing.

The danger of staying in this comfort zone is that although the present procedures practiced within the business entity are working well for the said business, the individual may be missing out on opportunities to further grow the business and make it leaps and bounds more successful.

Therefore understanding the merits of staying current through actively being involved in training programs, will help to keep all involved abreast with what are the latest tools, practices, innovations and other such advances available in the market today.

Some or all of these when applied to the various components of the current business environment will in most cases benefit the business either immediately or in the long run. There is also the cost saving point that some newer ideas may help to bring about.

Incorporating periodical training sessions will also help the individual understand what is currently going on in the business arena of the times.

This is especially important, as most home business entrepreneurs don't have the luxury of being in contact with the cooperate world as a whole, where such changes are apparent and constantly at the forefront for all to be privy to.

This is especially so, if the said business entity is not catering to this level, in its services or products.

Training programs also provide some outside interaction within the peers, where information and experiences can be discussed, exchanged and explored for the betterment of the business and its competing entities.

Ideas and new contacts can be made and new relationships can be formed through the training sessions, where like-minded individuals come together, for the common goal of learning something new.

Stay on Top of the Game through Promotions

Introducing promotions in an important way to reach the target audience in an effective and enticing manner, whereby the interest of the intended party is stirred to harness the possibility of making a commitment toward whatever that is being promoted.

Promotions have been noted to be among the more innovative ways of reaching the target audience effectively and with the shortest possible time frame.

This is of course a very important factor in the quest to garner the desired revenue to the business entity as a whole. Basically it is all about the business entity reaching out and communication with the potential customer bases.

The following are some avenues that should be explored within the promoting exercise for the home business entity:

Advertising – this is sometimes the more extensive and expensive way of getting the recognition for the product, service or business to the forefront of the intended audience.

For some this is an effective and quick way of getting product recognition, but it is also a costly way of doing so. Unless there is a budget for doing so, most home based businesses do not use this form of reaching the target audience too often.

Personal selling – being brave and skilled enough to approach anyone and everyone in order to promote the business, product or service is also another way of promoting the individual's company.

The personal selling technique is initially initiated through the developing of a relationship with the intended potential customer, which usually evolves into the ultimate goal of actually making a firm sale or commitment on the part of the customer.

Sales promotions – this is also another way to garner the committed interest of the target audience. The attractiveness of having the possibility of getting something with additions at no further cost is always well received.

Chapter 7- Relax and If Needed, Let Go

For most the anxiety starts to build when the perceived comfort and revenue is not forthcoming in the manner initially planned out and this can and will usually lead to stress and other negative elements encroaching into the mix. Therefore is it important to learn to incorporate some level of the relax state of mind when being faced with challenged through the course of the business exercise.

In the initial stages of the home business venture a good and proper time schedule should be drawn up that given the individual time to "breath" periodically during the actual working hours set aside.

This time is the used to relax and clear the mind, even if it is for a short period of time. Most people find this short break away for the physical surrounding of the work area does help to revitalize the individual and this of course contributes positively to the refreshed state of mind and body.

Taking time to relax does not necessary mean going on vacation, especially if the home business has only just started. It could mean taking time off for a few hours to touch base and exchange ideas with other like-minded business individual.

This in itself is refreshing as it would provide the individual with the vital link to the outside world and also connect to all the latest innovations available that may be of help to the business advancement possibilities.

Through this relaxing exercise the individual get to fill up on vital information that he or she may not have been privy to, being stuck at home immersed in the business activities of the day.

On Letting Go

"Wait!" you say! She's all the same interested as she still takes my calls. So does a prisoner in jail. And that's a very good comparison. Among the biggest errors made in home business: "Too many business owners spending too much time with too many individuals with too little interest."

The prospect has several different ways of stating that you need to go find somebody else, and perhaps later would be a good time to talk to me (or perhaps never) You must be mindful of these signs. If you see them then you might consider getting another prospect. You should be doing that in any event as you need to add a new individual in the pipeline daily!

What are these signs?

1) If the prospect abruptly becomes less than enthusiastic about speaking with you. You are able to feel it. It's the lack of energy on the telephone with you. Their energy drops from the first time you spoke. And if it continues to drop- they're being nice to you. But they've said nope already with the drop in energy- with every call.

2) If the prospect continues to say, "I've one more question…" That's code for — "I'm leading you on." Yes, there are those uncommon exceptions that some prospect wants to build an encyclopedia of data before making a decision- but it is one in 100. The rest are leading you on. Get another prospect. You don't need their torment or lack of esteem for you.

3) If the prospect continues to say…" nope I have not- but I will. I promise. I've been really busy." Busy for six months? Come on. Get real you're not busy. You're a jerk for not telling the networker nope. Let the networker know that you're not interested. And if they don't- YOU tell them nope. You're not in the business of letting somebody waste your time. Let them go- and find a fresh prospect. One that's honest and up front with you.

4) If the prospect phones you back- at uncanny hours and you only get their VM message. Prospects may be a trip. They may be truly canny at knowing when you're not going to be at home. And they call you to say they want you to continue giving chase to them! Don't. Your name isn't Fido. You don't chase after individuals. You're a business owner and are in the business of helping individuals- not chasing after them to satisfy their ego.

5) If the prospect carries on saying, "I'm still entertaining it." After four months- they're still thinking, and still supposing, then it's time to let them and all their thinking go.

Nancy Hall

Find a red-hot prospect that wants to do something with their life, and wants to do something today! You're seeking somebody whose timing is today and your business is correct for them. Clean your "Maybes" up and get them off the wall. If they won't be upfront and tell you nope- then you plainly help them along- and tell them nope. Keep in touch. Call them back from time to time. But that's only when you want to play The Great Prospect Chase Game again in your home business. You merit better. And so do your other prospects. They're waiting on you to call them.

ABOUT THE AUTHOR

Nancy Hall owns a cleaning business, which started from a home-based operation. Prior to her business, Nancy was a fulltime mother who was left to budget her husband's income as an office worker. Oftentimes, she had to sacrifice some things in order to pay for all their bills.

Tired of living on a very tight budget, Nancy taught herself the ins and outs of a home business. Today, she provides valuable insights tested by her experiences to other moms who want to better their families.

www.ingramcontent.com/pod-product-compliance
Lightning Source LLC
Chambersburg PA
CBHW051258170526
45165CB00004B/1766